To the Sene

Best wish

Virginia Tohr

DL-Said

17.3.2011

Mascat.

CW00517285

BANGING ON

A Bird's-Eye View of Country Sport

Piffa Schroder

Illustrated by Timothy Jaques

GUN ROOM PUBLISHING
47 Victoria Road, London W8 5RH

BANGING ON

First published 1990
by Ashford, Buchan & Enright

Republished 1995
by Gun Room Publishing
47 Victoria Road, London W8 5RH

British Library Cataloguing in Publication
Data. A CIP catalogue record for this book
is available from the British Library

ISBN 1 900284 00 6

Printed and bound by Biddles, Guildford
and King's Lynn

By the same author: *Fair Game: A Lady's
Guide to Shooting Etiquette*

Contents

Ruffled Feathers: A Bird's-Eye View   1

January: Comfort and Joy   7

February: Waidmann's Hell   12

March: Cry Havoc   16

April: Birds of a Feather   24

May: Hairy Marys   29

June: The Romance of Sport   33

July: Game for Anything   38

August I: A Legitimate Grouse   43

August II: Over the Hill   49

September: Covert in Confusion   56

October: Highland Fling   59

November: Two in the Bush   65

December: Eating Humble Pie   71

Last Word: Have Gun, Will Travel   76

Lock, Stock and Barrel:

    a glossary of sporting terms   82

To B. L. S.

My unbounded thanks to Tony Jackson, former editor of *Countrysport,* for having encouraged me to write for the magazine; and to Tim Jaques for his marvellous illustrations. And to Toby Buchan for his great help and enthusiasm.

A Bird's-Eye View

I'm always glad I didn't marry a man who liked morris dancing. It is of course one of the unspoken laws of marriage that, as a wife, you learn to accept, participate in and enjoy your husband's hobbies and sports. This may entail many years of tearing up the list of failed New Year's resolutions, and the end result, and the utter nobility of your achievements, may go completely unsung, but at least you have to try. It must be said that some hobbies are easier to deal with than others — budgies or model trains, for instance, are simple and merely require a good supply of ear-plugs. Vintage cars mean you have to wrap up warmly and be good at pouring tea from thermoses on the move; for golf you need strong ankles and an iron constitution to deal with jokes involving balls; for sailing you need to learn how to juggle in a cupboard and remember vital things like which is windward when you're going to be sick. Tennis and bridge are almost the worst of all, as you will be expected to partner at both and you can't fudge either. Shooting, however, is in a class of its own: it is by far the easiest sport to be married to since the only thing that, as a wife, you have to remember is — whatever the blandishments, however great the temptation of a lovely day out in the open, the good company, the fun — STAY AT HOME.

I once saw an advertisement headed 'For Shooting Wives'. This was, presumably, the same sort of journalese that produces headlines like 'Housewives Are Revolting' but, knowing the reaction with which most men greet the news that the wife is coming out for the day, it does make you think. Shooting is, after all, their sport and they resent female intruders, whom I think they always suspect of not taking the thing seriously enough; or maybe it is that women are a distraction for other men who might ogle their bird — as if one were wearing a badge saying 'Sex appeal — please give generously'. On the other hand, English men do love to have Sporting Wives; 'Game little woman, eh?' I heard one man say to another, as they rested comfortably on their shooting sticks after a particularly spectacular drive one cold winter's day, and opened their hip flasks. The only evidence of any such creature was a series of strangled cries for help emanating from a distant holly bush.

During one memorable winter shooting party in Scotland we had a lovely Saudi sheikh to stay, beautifully turned out in Huntsman's best and complete with bodyguards. He was wonderfully enthusiastic about the fact that everyone was allowed to take part in the sporting activities — women and children included — and although this was his first experience he had taken the trouble to go off to a shooting school first, and entered into the spirit of the thing with great gusto. He also prided himself on being a crack pistol shot, and the long-suffering bodyguards would be made to stand round on the lawn after Sunday breakfast with tin cans on their heads while he showed off his skills. The perfect hostess, I volunteered to join them, proving my utter faith both in his marksmanship and his integrity

as a guest. The other men of the party thought this frightfully sporting but the sheikh was horrified. He refused my offer, on the grounds that whereas back home he had lots of wives, so that one more or less would hardly signify, how could anyone with only one wife ('and she so fearless') even contemplate such a thing? This caused great amusement all round.

He had been educated at an English public school and then had been a Cambridge man, and so had spent all the requisite number of years learning to make toast and going beagling and hauling Morris Minors on to the Senate roof, and acquiring that particular brand of absolutely impeccable English that only foreigners can produce; but he had never been out shooting, and had therefore never had to grapple with that peculiar phenomenon, the well-trained wife of an English sporting gentleman. He also had a slight problem with certain terminology — innocuous things like, for instance, the words of endearment with which the English gentleman will address his wife. 'What is this silly old thing to which you keep referring?' he asked my husband one afternoon as everyone climbed back into the vehicles after the last drive of the day. On hearing the explanation, he was aghast. 'But my dear fellow, this is preposterous: we may be barbarians, but at least we are civilised barbarians. I would shoot any man who referred to even one of my wives in such terms.'

It occurred to me that his wives, even if they were allowed to watch him shoot, were probably not expected to do most of the things that an English wife happily learns to take in her stride as part of the unspoken marriage vows, nor would they have enjoyed the experience, and I endeavoured to explain the ritual of the thing a little. I said that any lady who is invited to go shooting with her husband in this country is of course aware of the honour and privilege thus accorded to her, and will do her utmost to ensure that her behaviour conforms to the rigorous codes laid down, by gentlemen, for such an occasion. Her husband will naturally behave with the impeccable courtesy which is his wont. At all times the complete gentleman, he will be affable and amiable, he will do everything in his power to ensure that she enjoys the day; he will help her over stiles and under wires; he will enquire solicitously about her well-being; he will invite her to stand with him, if she is so minded, and will be as gallant, charming, amusing and considerate as if he were caring for his aged nanny, or another man's wife.

No English gentleman, I went on — warming to my task — would jump up and down, red-faced and foaming, should his wife inadvertantly happen to drop his open cartridge bag; he would never send her to pick up in places where he himself would not dream of going, or then bawl at her when she is a couple of fields away 'No no no not THERE, no you FOOL, good God woman didn't you MARK it . . .' He would not on any account make venomous remarks concerning her appearance, or her abilities, within the hearing of anyone else; and a gentleman would never, ever, name his dog after one of his wife's ex-lovers, however much satisfaction he might derive from thrashing it publicly. In short, I told him, an English gentleman in the shooting field is, as any wife will testify, the epitome of all that is finest and most noble in mankind.

The sheikh's bread-and-butter letter arrived the following week. 'I have been seriously considering all that I learnt during my stay with you,' it read 'and have come to the conclusion that English women are the incarnation of angels in this mortal sphere.' When the prolonged — and to my mind rather unnecessary — screams of laughter had subsided, it was discovered that my husband had managed to crack a rib. It seemed, under the circumstances, curiously appropriate.

Comfort and Joy

Christmas comes and goes, leaving one feeling more or less bleary-eyed than usual; but in Scotland the really important festival is Hogmanay. In *Webster's Third International Dictionary*, the word 'Hogmanay' is defined as: 'Scot.: 1) New Year's Eve; 2) traditional celebration at New Year's Eve; a) the going about of children from house to house singing and asking for gifts usually of cakes or nuts'.

Now I know (because it says so at the front) that this dictionary has been compiled 'using all the experience and resources of more than one hundred years', but it was printed in Chicago, and maybe they are not completely *au fait* there with the Hogmanay We Know Here. In the Highlands and Islands for instance, where Hogmanay is the prime festival of the year, the ceremony of going about from house to house asking for gifts has absolutely nothing to do with children, cakes or nuts. It has to do with distilleries, and the end product thereof. One particular island boasts nine of the things and therefore it can be assumed that Hogmanay, as celebrated thereon, is a fairly simple affair, consisting as it does of grown men going round demanding hospitality from as many houses as possible throughout the hours of darkness (loosely referred to as 'We'll just be poppin' by in the evenin''), and taking on board any given quantity — this phrase is not used loosely — of the local amber nectar. It is therefore quite logical to assume

January

that any event taking place within the subsequent twenty-four hours is bound to be, in the words of the Irish sage, a complete state of chassis.

Any New Year's Day shoot starts off, in these parts, fairly late. It is not that the house party has been out, but rather that the locals have been in — 'first-footing' — and by the time that the last one has been steered, full of good cheer and clutching his regulation bit of shortcake, into the first light of dawn, everyone is feeling just the merest bit fragile over breakfast. There are no beaters or keepers around, of course, the whole thing is in the hands of the host who looks like the Wrath of God, and the first drive (anything under the age of fourteen is frog-marched into the rhododendrons to do some work) is a disaster. Nothing at all comes out until the final moment when there is an explosion of small boys and spaniels, all called Ben, from the undergrowth, who then have to be collared and thrashed to heel. Someone has thoughtfully brought out the King's Ginger and there's also some rather good fruit cake; and the distillery manager who has joined up by now has also very generously brought a large bottle, mysteriously labelled Iron-Bru, for everyone's consumption; so tempers are restored and the decision finally made to walk up the woods to Woodcock Corner, as long as someone drives a vehicle round to the other end. Progress is slow, punctuated by strangled shouts of 'Over' and 'Yours' — nobody wants to let their gun off lest their head fall off too — and a voice can be heard in deep cover reciting Stuart-Wortley in lugubrious tones — the bit that starts off 'After an almost sleepless night breakfast will revolt your feverish eye' and goes on about 'that peculiar class of head which feels after each shot like the opening and shutting of a heavy book, charged with electricity'.

Sometimes we would instead go flighting the geese, having not bothered to go to bed at all. Usually we would be joined by one of the neighbours, a splendid rather crippled old general who always brought his butler out shooting. The butler would appear with two small chamois-leather bags hanging from his belt, one for the extra-strong mints to which the general was particularly partial after a heavy night, and one for the general's false teeth. As the first birds came over, the general would cast aside his sticks in the manner of one miraculously cured, give a rallying cry of 'Steady the Buffs now Hendridge', and the butler would step forward smartly and hold him up for the shot.

On one occasion we had with us a firearms enthusiast who had just acquired an ancient 4-bore with which he was determined to fire at least one shot. It was unfortunate that he happened to be standing on a particularly boggy bit as the birds flew over, but he did get his goose even though he hadn't reckoned on the recoil and had to be rescued before he had disappeared altogether.

One year we decided to go hind stalking on New Year's Day. Things got off to a pretty bad start as we had to drive back to the house, twice — once for the rifles, once for the ammunition — and then the keeper fell over his garden gate when we finally arrived to collect him. He then sat in the back of the steaming Land-Rover, smiling horribly with a glazed expression in the eyes, motionless and in total silence except during the moments when we drove over the cattle-grids, when he would hold his head and moan. Finally we set off up the hill, the keeper following mournfully behind, crunching over the frosty ground. Every step seemed to echo for miles. Occasionally we would come to a rather untidy halt and take a spy, only to see groups of beasts staring, then trotting away into the distance. 'Perhaps we're not doing this too well' someone suggested after a couple of hours' fruitless slog. 'Why don't we go home and have a little nap?' So we did.

Waidmann's Hell

When you're sitting all huddled together in the shooting vehicle, bouncing over the ruts leading to the next drive, and the frightfully good-looking man sitting next to you turns to the man on his other side and lisps smugly: 'Gary'th got a *lovely* thoft mouth', he is (usually) only talking about his dog.

It's all to do with buzz-words. Terminology in any sphere is the greatest pitfall for the uninitiated, and the world of country sports is no exception. Someone ought to write a handbook for idiots like me who haven't yet learned the jargon: I went rabbiting on for years about 'left-and-rights' for instance, completely unaware that that is a boxing term and that the correct shooting phrase is a 'right-and-left'; and people get very cross and look as if you'd uttered an obscenity if you get it wrong.

These same people, on the other hand, do come out themselves with the most astonishing phrases, obviously part of the esoteric plot — and you are supposed to know what it means. 'There's some more of those damned Frenchmen' roared an angry brigadier in the middle of a Suffolk field. I hadn't noticed any and was about to volunteer to help out in my best Lycée French when someone mercifully set me right. I then asked, naïvely I now realise, how on earth you could tell the difference between one sort of partridge and another in the air. 'That's easy' came the withering reply.

12

13

'Englishmen come together.' Woe betide you if you even blink.

If it is difficult, in your own country and your own language, to learn the correct jargon, it is doubly so when you go abroad (and for that matter, think of poor foreigners who come here to shoot) when you haven't a clue as to what might be the correct form: not walking over dead game, for instance, or how to accept the *Waidmannsheil* gracefully from your host when you have finally managed to fell a boar, or a roe, or a red deer. I was explaining this nice custom to a Scottish keeper one day as we both heaved and struggled to pull a dead stag out of a particularly nasty bit of bog. 'Aye, but we've got a better custom here for when we've shot a beast: we just go home and take a bloody great dram.'

The first time I ever shot anything abroad was in Holland, where very kindly I had been invited to shoot a roe near the Hoge Veluwe. Knowing that I would spend the whole day alone with one of the local keepers, and not knowing a single word of Dutch, I'd spent the previous week in agonies of nerves and a dictionary, noting down words for relevant phrases like 'I cannot see the animal you refer to' and 'It is impossible to shoot through this tree' and 'I am very sorry' and 'Please may I lie down now', as well as numbers up to ten and the words for yes and no, right and left, thank you so much, no don't worry it was completely my fault, and what a wonderful day. (Think of going hind stalking, on some remote Scottish hill, with a keeper in full spate: 'C'mon girrul, ye can see her cleere as cleere now, the beast behind that big yellow bitch there scratching her backside, third from the left up beyond that wee knoll to the right of the scree, and fer God's sake watch out for that nobber . . .' Then translate into Dutch, using only one side of the paper . . .)

On the appointed day I flew out from Heathrow, arrived at Schiphol, located the driver who had been sent to collect me, and, for the next two hours as we drove through the dank early morning mists, sat in the back of the car with a torch and my Notes for Little Linguists, rehearsing my carefully prepared words. The driver, who spoke no English, must have thought he had a lunatic on board. Finally, after quite a lot of map-reading and Satanic mutterings and stops to peer through the maze of unsigned roads and deep unhelpful stretches of woods, we arrived at the keeper's house. The car crunched on the gravel, the front door opened and out he came, boots and loden jacket and a face like a truckle bed, accompanied by one of those nice brown hunting dogs. I swallowed hard and clambered out of the car and, smiling in what I fondly hoped was a relaxed, easy-going, Dutch-speaking fashion, held out my hand, trying to remember if the accent fell on the first or second syllable of 'Good . . .' The truckle bed opened up welcomingly into a huge grin. 'Morning ma'am, had a nice drive? It sure is a pig's ear of a place to find, I guess you're just longing for some good hot carfee . . .'

He'd spent the war washing up at the Air Force base near Enschede, and learning pure, mellifluous, wonderful, marvellous, magically fluent Brooklynese.

Cry Havoc

I once met a man who said he always found it particularly helpful to thrash his dog *before* a day's shooting,
in order to Make It Mind. This was, apparently, a legacy
from his public school days when, he explained, he
himself had been beaten quite regularly for exactly the
same reason (or else for General Attitude, which came
to much the same thing) and it didn't seem to have
done him any harm. The dog certainly never took un-
due offence nor, it must be said, did it behave one whit
better as a result. This form of dog-management was,
however, in marked contrast to that of a friend who
came to stay, bringing with him his aged and completely uncontrollable labrador bitch; throughout every
drive, as she squealed and whined and rushed about, he
could be heard enquiring dolefully 'Sandy, WILL you
behave?' Sandy climbed unchided onto every chair in
the house, apparently on some preconceived rota basis
of her own devising, and one evening was happily laid
out in an old pale leather armchair in the study. Somebody went to move her whereupon she looked up, with
a vacuous but not unpleasant expression on her face,
and peed — slowly, and at length. Conversation ground
to a halt and we all watched in fascination as she went
on and on. When she had finished she heaved herself
down to the floor and went off to find another dry
chair, while I set off to find her owner. 'O girlie' came a
plaintive voice, 'how COULD you?'.

16

Things brightened up a bit the next day when another member of the party, an extremely sporting bishop, asked if he could borrow Sandy for one of the drives 'just to help out a bit'. At the end of the drive everyone was picking up and there was no sign of the bishop. Suddenly the most appalling yelping came from the depths of the undergrowth, and a stentorian voice was heard shouting delightedly 'Ha, that'll teach you, you stupid great bitch'. He swore afterwards that he had never touched her and it had been merely a slight misunderstanding between them, but she had somehow ended up in the middle of a holly bush. She behaved impeccably for the rest of the day.

I was brought up in an Irish houseful of mixed breeds — soppy boxers who took sugar in their bowls of tea, a nice lurcher who smiled a lot, an awful pink bull-terrier that bit everything in sight, two rather serious labradors and an evil old spaniel whom I loathed. As a child, holidays involved ritual visits to relations round the country, the most keenly anticipated of which was to a favourite and bed-ridden great-uncle in Wicklow. Wearing a rather fine Turkish cap with a tassel, he would puff his way through endless Passing Clouds and drink whiskey from a silver cup as he lay propped up against mountains of pillows carving bits of wood. The best moment was when the doctor arrived on his daily round, whereupon my uncle would gleefully pull back his bedclothes and reveal the pair of greyhounds who lived down there permanently. He claimed, quite logically it seemed to me, that they kept his feet warm.

Later on in life I had an Alsatian, a red setter which was found on the doorstep with a note tied to its collar

saying 'Sorry, we're off to America, good luck' and, in London, a marvellous Battersea hound which had obviously been city-flat-trained to go on paper. The daily delivery of mail and news through the letter-box meant a horrendous start to every morning until we finally realised and nailed up a basket inside the front door.

At Oxford I had been introduced to beagling, and fell deeply in love with the Master from the moment I first saw him carrying out a huge laundry basket which he opened up on its side on the lawn, and a couple of dozen fat puppies spilled out like honey over the grass. The romance came to naught but hounds of any sort always retained a special magic ever after. In the *Sporting Magazine* of 1828, an article refers to the Keswick pack of hounds as 'as fierce as a tiger, as long as a hayband, but with an amicable cast of features like the Chancellor of the Exchequer'. The most endearing foxhound I ever met was one who, since his paternity was in some doubt, had been removed from the hunt kennels to be brought up by the Master with the rest of his own dogs. His greatest joy was being taken out for a day's shooting: he was hopeless at retrieving but runners never stood a chance although, once reached, he didn't know what to do with them, so would sit on them, wearing that rather nice expression that only a hound can produce, until help came.

My father had a pack of dachshunds as a young man in India: there were sixteen of them, and one of them apparently went for a tiger — which must have been surprised — and came happily trotting back disgorging fur and totally unscathed. I used to think that dachshunds were merely harmless and weak-bladdered; but

19

that they can be fierce little things is proved by the wire-haired variety used at boar shoots on the Continent, hardy and tough as nails, urged on to follow up wounded animals with strident cries of '*Attaque, attaque*' by terrifying women in long boots and green hats, who then encourage the dogs to savage the dead carcases. You want to watch your ankles, as they go for anything that moves. We were shooting in Germany one day and a Belgian, standing beside the body of the huge boar he had shot, was being clapped on the shoulder and congratulated by everyone. He stepped forward to receive his *Waidmannsheil* from the host whereupon a small furry bottlebrush hurled itself at his leg with a howl of triumph and latched on. The women in green hats laughed like hyenas, the wretched man hopped round on one leg screeching invectives and trying to dislodge the dog who, obviously under the impression that he was doing a grand job in the face of fearful odds, hung on relentlessly, everyone was yelling instructions and there was blood everywhere, when suddenly an Italian shouted 'STANDA STEEL, I WILL SHOOT EEM OFF' and raised his double-barrelled rifle. One of the women in a green hat started to scream and the rest of the party threw themselves to the ground as if poleaxed. The dog, realising it had managed to bring down its quarry in the most exemplary fashion, let go, spat out bits of sock and flesh, wagged its tail and looked round for acclamation. Next day, everyone came out in knee-length boots.

The English woman and the dog has of course been one of the great ongoing love stories of all time. Most English females could admit that — shades of *Love in a*

21

Cold Climate — their first love had been canine, but it continues well beyond childhood. A normally sane and rational girlfriend of mine, callously rejected by her suitor, nevertheless continued to look after his labrador whilst he was off gallivanting with Others. *For a year.* When I suggested that really the Time Had Come, and perhaps what she should do was encourage the dog to roll in something very dead then take it round that evening to the ex-suitor's house where the dastardly fellow would be no doubt busily ensconced in his latest *trouvaille*, then ring the bell and leave, she was horrified. 'But I couldn't do that,' she cried miserably, 'Libby *hates* going out at night'.

When such devotion takes place in your own family, however, it's no laughing matter. My eight-year old daughter was given a puppy one Christmas by an enthusiastic — and to my mind totally deranged — godfather. The house was bedlam anyway, by midday everyone was beginning to feel a little frail, but it was decided to let the puppy join the party for half an hour before lunch. (Enthusiasts should here refer to *Training Gundogs*, Chapter 1: 'You will be entering a new way of life, one from which there is no escape.') Within seven minutes the puppy had gardened its way with enormous enthusiasm through most of the presents under the tree, savaged odd bits of fluff on the carpet, upended an ancient relative, twice, and felled the firescreen, and was also by now an astonishing shade of emerald green having pounced on and then eaten a large amount of coloured tissue paper. Then, quite suddenly, everything was still. 'Where is it?' we all screamed in panic. My daughter crawled out happily from behind a sofa, her eyes shining. 'Don't worry' she said 'he's *perfectly* alright now, he's just been sick'; and I knew her first love affair had begun.

Birds of a Feather

How nice it would be, I thought one day — looking at photographs of the Game Fair at Chantilly — to be French. Especially to be a French woman out shooting in France. Shooting in France (or anywhere else on the Continent for that matter) is a totally different matter to shooting in Great Britain, and French women seem to have a distinct edge over their British counterparts: they appear relaxed, chatting and laughing with the men around them, chic, glamorous, elegant and attractive; they have flair and panache; their clothes are beautifully made and beautifully worn and are a credit to their designers. They make English women in the same situation look like country bumpkins. Why?

It has nothing to do with the availability of good clothes in this country, nor obviously has it anything to do with the basic difference between the French female shape (small waists and cherry bottoms) and the English Pear; and it is ridiculous to suppose that British women are not just as fashion-conscious as their French counterparts when London is bracketed with Paris, Milan and New York as a fashion centre of the West. So why do we have to look like the Wrath of God on the shooting field?

There can be only one answer: men.

This is not a sexist remark: I do not mean men in general, I mean *English* men, as opposed to, let us say, French men. A Frenchman loves anything to do with *la chasse*, whether it be of beasts or of beauties, and the fact that he is out for a day to kill the one will not preclude him from chatting up the other. Frenchmen LOVE women; they love the whole idea of women; they are delighted to be seen with good-looking ones, they love to talk to them, to flirt with them; they enjoy their company on every occasion, sporting or otherwise; they recite '*Les Quatre-Vingt Chasseurs*' with gusto and relish; and the women know that, to maintain this admirable state of affairs, they must always look attractive, alluring and irresistible, whether in the bushes or the boudoir. Being dab hands at the psychological game, they always appear beautifully turned out and dressed to kill, which gives a lot of pleasure all round.

English men, on the other hand, are chauvinists. English men consider that shooting, rather like the erstwhile Church of England, is something run by gentlemen *for* gentlemen. Where Frenchmen like to talk to their women before (and during) drives, English men like to talk to each other or to their dogs. There is only one thing an Englishman dislikes more than a woman when he is out shooting, and that is an obviously attractive, glamorous, FEMININE woman. If there must be a female around at such times, it should be uncontroversial, willing, obedient and useful, and preferably labrador.

It therefore follows that if and when an Englishman does allow a woman to accompany him out shooting, he will prove his mastery of the situation by laying down perfectly clear rules beforehand as to what she may and may not do. 'If you come out, you come out to help; do NOT talk during drives, do NOT interfere, do NOT

26

offer half-witted suggestions, and do NOT turn up looking like some damned foreigner with feathers in your
hat.' His woman, like his dog, is there for function not
adornment, and unless she is prepared to assist him, to
load, mark, retrieve, pick up, keep tally, praise and
work, then she can stay behind. This being so, why
should she dress up?

He will therefore condemn the fashionable as 'un-
British' and the attractive as 'bad form'; and because,
by and large, English women tolerate most of what their
men throw at them, they will obey instructions rather
than suffer the humiliation of being sent off the field. I
remember once dressing 'differently' for a winter day's
shoot, in a lovely old pair of leather culottes, a brown
loden cape, a wonderfully ancient hat of my father-in-
law's with a cock feather in it, and one of those good
Belgian shooting muffs lined with beaver; the women
looked nervous, the men looked appalled, and the 'My-
goodness-don't-you-look-smart' was not intended as a
compliment, either. Women in the British shooting
arena are not meant to look smart; unlike their French
sisters, they are there for expediency, not for
decoration.

So the whole question of dress really comes down to
two points: the man's idea of the role of women in the
shooting field, and what he demands of them. There is
no way in which a really beautiful outfit (however correct it may be) is going to look good when its wearer is
sent to pick up in a thorn bush, or is dispatched to
retrieve some dead thing from the middle of the river
— hence the unisex cords, wellies etc. which are the
accepted 'uniform' for the thing. It is not that English

women do not have the nerve (or the inspiration, or the suppliers, or the initiative) to look chic out shooting: it is that the men — for whom and by whom, after all, the sport was originally invented, and who must therefore maintain their superiority in all matters concerning it — have decreed that it is somehow 'wrong' for a woman to turn up in anything other than the uniform they approve of, a working garb devoid of any hint of sexuality, and designed (by other men) to be practical, hard-wearing and tough — qualities they expect from the wearers as well.

Only when an Englishman realises that his undoubted superiority in the shooting field cannot possibly be threatened by a feather, or that his standing amongst his peers will not crumble (it might even, just possibly, be enhanced) if he is accompanied by a chic companion; only then will he be able to relax, and she will be allowed to look as elegant in the shooting field as she does out of it. And the dog will be left in peace to attend to the serious business of picking-up.

Hairy Marys

In Ireland, you could always tell the fishing fraternity by its forearms. Nothing to do with muscle or circumference, just the colour — that wonderful rich crinkly deep mahogany which came to an abrupt end round about the elbows. One hot summer, we took a stretch of the Blackwater. Smart neighbours would turn up for drinks in the balmy evenings, the women in sleeveless dresses wearing dusty diamonds and what appeared to be long alligator gloves.

Later on in the year the talk might be of the rigours of the Duhallow Hunt Ball, and who had broken their neck or why they hadn't, but during the summer the only subject of conversation was fish. Over the Waterford crystal, delicate little old ladies of seventy-plus with faces the hue of aborigines would discuss 'killing salmon' and 'a moderate sort of beast' (anything over 16 pounds was rated moderate); and down in Fermoy, where the general merchant still boasted one of those ancient banking systems where you put the money in a metal canister and whizzed it across to the till on an overhead line, all trade would stop when anyone came in to buy fishing gear. The whole populace would gather round to discuss and to give advice.

One disastrous week, the fish weren't taking anything at all, it seemed. 'Sure if you was to be givin' dem de winnin' sweepstake ticket wid yer own hand, dey still wouldn't be takin' it', the coal-merchant announced. 'A coupla sticks of doinamite might do the job though'. 'Aren't you the unlucky one now, didn't Father Ryan just walk out now wid the last ones' came a shout from the back of the shop. Amidst the laughter, another group was arguing as to the reason for the salmon's reluctance to be caught: 'It's dem tings dat go round and round in de Atalantic, dey's making great holes in the atmosfur' ventured one, a keen meteorologist. But someone else had the answer: 'Not at all, ye great goon; it's de otthers; de place is *walkin*' wid otthers'.

As a child, I would watch the fish flying up the salmon leap at Leixlip and was shown by the *garda* — my mentor in many matters — how to tickle them in the bit of the Rye water that ran through the woods below the house. Every week during the season, the mentor would come and present the household with a nice fat salmon and would be liberally rewarded for his work with a couple of hours' worth of 'refreshment', until it was discovered that the fish had of course been poached from our own water. Another fine fisherman was, as seems to be the tradition in such communities, the local priest. His fishing-rod lived permanently at an angle beside the confessional and, during the fishing months, he would give Benediction in his gumboots so as not to lose a minute before the evening rise. He had a nice line in home-made flies of his own indeterminate design but of fiendish efficacy, to each of which a blessing would be imparted before its first cast, and which were known — inevitably — as 'Hell Marys'.

One year, thanks to the fact that my father had had his driving licence temporarily removed after a small argument with a bollard in the village, we had a chauffeur called Murphy. He also doubled up as butler and gardener, and rapidly took over most of the odd jobs around the house, including that of feeding the hens until one magical evening when they were found crooning softly and swaying around the hen-house, when it transpired that he had added whiskey to their feed. He took over as my mentor, taught me to cast standing on the kitchen table, and instructed me in many things which young ladies should know, including how to spread mustard and hot water over the ground to facilitate the collection of worms. He played the fiddle like an angel and used to take me mushrooming in the early dew, his fiddle at the ready to play to any of the little folk we happened to see. He made the most wonderful poteen, a saucer of which had also to be left outside for the little folk to ensure their co-operation, but he never explained to me why, when I went down to investigate the saucer one snowy morning, the little folk wore such big boots.

Murphy gave me my first fishing lessons, but it wasn't until many years later that I learned how patient and diplomatic such teachers are. 'You're doing grand altogether, mum' would come the laconic comment from one ghillie after another, as I hurled great heaps of knitting into the river and wondered why nothing ever happened. And then came the memorable day on the Laggan when, after a really hairy display of ineptitude from the bank, I managed to lose the first salmon I'd ever managed to get on to a line, to be comforted by the generous words: 'Ca' canny, lass, you were doing fine, fine, it was only a pity the bridge came by just then and got in the way.'

A friend told me the story of how she caught her first salmon as a child in Scotland. She and the ghillie had arrived back very late at the house, her father had gone down to greet them and, amazed at the size of the fish lying out on the table, asked the ghillie how on earth his daughter had managed, as they had been out in the boat. 'Well sir,' came the reply, 'it was a combined effort, as you might say. I told the young lady to hold on with both hands, and I just rowed the bugger round and round until he died.'

The Romance of Sport

June is, traditionally, the month of romance, a word encompassing not only love — like Burns's 'red, red rose that's newly sprung in June'— but also, if you look at the dictionary, such things as chivalry, archaic poems and 'extravagant fictions', or 'an attraction or aspiration of an emotional or romantic nature'. It also mentions phrases like the romance of steel and steam, the romance of whaling, and the romance of sport.

I once asked a keeper what he thought of the romance of sport. A small extremely dour Scotsman, with the face of one who might well ask for vegetarian Alka-Seltzer if offered a drink, he was unbelievably married to a delicious cosy rosy-cheeked woman who kept goats in the front parlour, and to whom he invariably referred as 'the auld bitch'. He gave the question only cursory thought: 'Aye well, it's fair enough the romance for them as has the time, so long as it disna interfere with the sport.'

Typical chauvinist, I thought. A far cry from Diana of the Chase, Hesketh Pritchard or Bahram that Great Hunter. What about the wild hills of stalking days, the magical early mornings waiting for roe in bluebell woods, the roding woodcock in the cathedral of dusk, the peace of a river bank at sunset? Therein surely romance lies . . .

But then perhaps it all depends, too, on what you mean by sport. Back to the dictionary. 'Sport is sweetest

33

when there are no spectators', according to one pro-verb. 'Sport is amorous dalliance'. But this is, surely, a different kind of sport? 'Sport of kings', or 'sporting chance' is nearer the mark, as is 'a good sportsman'. But think of sporting ladies, and you're back to Amaryllis in the shade again.

I was once proposed to in a grouse butt — an inci-dent I have always regarded as deeply romantic — by a man whose estate tweed was of so glorious and flatter-ing a hue that I was almost minded to accept his offer. But you have to keep a sense of priorities as a female, however romantically inclined. Then there was a Nor-wegian, whose sporting suggestion that we should go and shoot bear in Northern Mongolia sounded irresiti-bly romantic until he added 'And ve vill naturally be sharing a yurt', and that was the end of that. And an-other incident I remember all too clearly involved standing deep in a wood for what seemed like an in-ordinately long drive, skipping round trees in an effort to dissuade an elegant and heavily-pomaded Italian whose astounding sexual proclivities, of which I had been warned by a thoughtful hostess, made the *Lays of Ancient Rome* sound like the title of his autobiography.

There is of course, as every sporting wife will appreci-ate, a world of difference between the romance *of* sport and romance *in* sport. Whereas all of them will extol the former, by and large the latter is not undertaken in this country by the male of the species. It is, as far as most of them are concerned, relegated to the odd, deeply significant moment when he shares his flask with you when you can't utter because of the cold, or even — a real triumph — holding hands in a shooting muff

when he's forgotten his gloves. (Englishmen are more noticeably *friendly*, in a sporting setting, in cold weather.) But then to be fair, not all of sporting life is 'romantic' in the poetic meaning of the word. Four o'clock in the morning, the rain is belting down, he's got a hangover on top of his midlife crisis, the old paper cartridges he found in his jacket have got stuck in the breeches, he's missed the only chance at greylag and has discovered, too late, that he's been sitting in a cowpat; this is not your state-of-the-art romantic hero figure. Nor is it the moment to go wittering on about the beauty of the sunrise. As a general rule of thumb (it may be interesting to note at this point that the phrase originated in the 1700s, when Judge Buller passed a judgment on wife-beating: it was perfectly acceptable, he said, for a man to beat his wife, provided he used a stick no thicker than his thumb) — as a general rule of thumb if you are searching for romance in a sporting setting, steer clear of sporting men. Women may be deemed fair game, and it's fine to chat up the birds in the shooting field and indulge in a little light banter with the odd female, but never forget that men are there for the romance of sport, not for the sport of romance.

Perhaps too, though, what is known as the romance of a sport is sometimes only romanticism — the setting, the situation, the perfection of a single moment in nature; the sight of a hundred red deer on a sunny hillside, the idea of fishing for sea trout by moonlight — and you then remember, belatedly, that your boots don't fit, or that the prophylactic effect of midges can never be underestimated. The business of the thing is often at odds with its romance, in sport as in the rest of life. If you think about it, a declaration of true love can take as little as three words; I read the other day that whereas the Lord's Prayer is made up of 56 words, the Ten Commandments of 297, and the American Declaration of Independence 300, the EEC, for its directive on the export of duck eggs, needs 26,911. There must be a moral in this somewhere.

Game for Anything

In the days of King John, a squirrel could travel from the Severn to the Humber without touching ground. This rather esoteric fact always gives me especial pleasure when motoring. I don't know how long the squirrel would have taken to make the journey, but it was probably much the same amount of time as we all take every year getting to the Game Fair. It seems to be one of the unheralded laws of life that, however near the Game Fair is to your own bit of country, the time you will spend snarled up in queues of traffic before finally exploding through the gates will be approximately three-and-a-half times longer than if you had driven to it from the other end of the kingdom.

Along with hundreds of thousands of others, I spent many years going to the Game Fair as a visitor. It is always a wonderful day's sport. You reckon the time you're going to need getting there, multiply by the year of your birth etc., etc., and set off, the car ladened with emergency rations, shooting sticks, comfortable shoes and a large soft basket in which to carry round purchases, loo paper and smelling salts. You return home that night wearier, hoarser, poorer and what feels like 3 feet shorter, but content. In 1988, for the first time, I went as a player.

They did tell me afterwards that, rather like the Crash of '87, if you managed to survive the Game Fair of '88 you could survive anything. It was certainly not the fault of the organisers, it was simply the fault of the weather: it poured and it poured and it poured for three days and the beautiful grounds of Floors Castle were churned and pulped to mud — thick, sticky gukky mud higher up, deep oily slow-flowing knee-high mud on the lower ground. The sun came out occasionally, then it rained again. The players would tramp into their stands by 9 am where they would remain incarcerated and shivering for the rest of the day, only making the occasional Oates-like sortie in case of dire emergency or desperation. The nobs and knockers would stomp in saying things like 'Jolly rotten luck, what?' and, taking one look round the sodden, filthy and splattered stand, would wait hopefully to be given a drink whilst treading in more muck and then, merrily waving their umbrellas and hanging onto their wader braces, would dive out into the quagmire again. Tractors churned about and got stuck, the loudspeaker kept on making horrific announcements about river banks or their demise. The players would look longingly at their watches, praying it was 6 o'clock when they could shut up shop, batten down the canvas and go away and drown their sorrows until the following morning, when once again they had to tramp back on to the stands . . . It was like a battlefield. The final insult came on the last evening when a gale blew up and made off with the tea-tent, and all the rubbish that had been carefully bagged up into skips got hurled up to the heavens and then flung into the surrounding trees.

Come to think of it, '88 was generally not so hot for country shows wherever you happened to be. The Puskar camel fair in Rajasthan was broken up by rioting camels, at San Fermín they had double the usual number of broken bones during the bull-running, and on the first day of the Rurál in Buenos Aires the President, who'd come to make a speech about agricultural improvements, got stoned by the farmers. As the Rurál takes place in the centre of the city, in an area about twice the size of Wembley Stadium, and everyone (but everyone) goes on the first day and the place is alive with television cameras, this was deemed by the government to be a Bad Thing.

The fact that the President was there at all proves the sort of show it is. The finest livestock of Argentina are paraded and tethered in great halls for inspection — the chunky fox-coloured *criollo* gaucho ponies in all their trappings, the sheep, the llamas and the cattle — and there are, too, the halls of produce stalls, leather, wines, cheese and meat. It is in a sense much the same as an English show, except that the cattle and sheep are approximately twice the size of any cattle or sheep you've ever seen (rather like the steaks, come to think of it), and every so often somebody sets about somebody else and tries to kill him, which is the way that little local grievances are sorted out. The smart set (who don't go in for this sort of thing but who bet heavily on the outcome), the estate owners and their friends, gather in El Hereford — a bar to one side of the cattle hall — for lunch: everyone wears a hat, and kisses everyone else (except presumably the President) to cries of 'Che, *como est*as, *que fantastico*', and the women call all the men '*amoroso*'.

On the second day, of course (it being '88), it poured, an unprecedented catastrophe, but by then the smart set had gone and so had the television crews, so it

40

didn't matter. Huge woolly sheep the size of Morris Minors were dragged protesting by very small boys round the sodden judging ring and horses splashed over the jumps through lakes of mire. Even the gauchos, glorious in red neckerchiefs, silver belts and black hats, looked despondent, their huge baggy pants hanging in heavy folds, like wet spaniel's ears, over their boots. But morale was generally high: a few really worthwhile fights had broken out, a couple with an old windup gramophone was dancing the tango in the llama hall, and the vendors of hideously undercooked *chorizo* hot-dogs were doing good business, and shouting lewd and cheerful comments to some of the young prostitutes who'd wandered in for the afternoon. The goat show was going well, if acridly, the produce hall seemed to have developed into some sort of private party where everyone stood with their arms round each other singing; and in the middle of an impassioned plea over the loudspeaker for Don Luis to kindly return to the collecting ring, with his horse, the announcer broke off to whistle at a very pretty girl walking past the commentary box. The audience turned, saw and cheered, to cries of 'Che, *paquetíssima*'.

That was the other nice thing about the Rurál. For the Latin-American man there is no moment in life, whatever he happens to be doing at the time, that is not enhanced by the sight of a woman. If you happen to be one, it does great things for the morale. In this country of course things are done rather differently, and should you happen to hear whistling at, say the Game Fair, *do not panic*: it will only be that the dog trials have started nearby.

A Legitimate Grouse

In England it is known, with a nod of respect towards the racing fraternity, as a Triple Crown, in Scotland as a Macnab. Whatever the terminology, the achievement of bagging a stag, a salmon and a brace of grouse all in the same day is not given to many, and is the cause for much celebration of a liquid nature that evening (come to think of it, this applies to almost anything north of the Border). I'll certainly never get one, mainly I suppose because I'm really hopeless at fishing and I couldn't catch a salmon if my life depended on it. I like watching people fish, I love eating the result, and I love being on a river bank on a sunny day, but I can't be doing with all those knots. In latter years, I've had an even better reason for never having had a Triple Crown, namely the demise of the grouse from our bits of the hill, although there are still the odd coveys purring away and ruining a good stalk (which augurs well enough for the Macnab enthusiasts). Meanwhile we have instituted the Triple Crown Second Class, which consists of a roe buck, a couple of trout and a brace of rock pigeon, which is equally as sporting as you have to stand up in a small heaving boat under the sea cliffs in order to get the rock pigeon, and not get caught up in the lobster creels while you're doing it.

I have a lovely photograph of my grandmother on a grouse moor somewhere, wielding a gun in what looks to be the most exemplary fashion; and the albums are

43

full of pictures of huge shooting parties, and wizened old keepers in enormous plus-fours and caps, with the birds all laid out in front of the game cart. Those were of course the Good Old Days when, after the pressures of standing round in a grouse butt while thousands of birds flew over, you would call 'BOY' during a lull in the proceedings and a smartly-clad helper, of tender years, would appear as if by magic bearing a bottle of Bollinger. Therefter of course it was known as 'calling for the Boy', by which name the champagne became known amongst the *cognoscenti*; geriatric old men, of whom there are plenty on any moor in August, still hark back wistfully to such memories.

Our grouse shooting consisted of walked-up birds — three weeks' worth of a lot of exercise and a huge amount of fun. Wherever you are, in Scotland or on the moors in Yorkshire, August is magic with the 'larks singing and the heather in bloom' (to quote a fine old shot, who used to recite the same Magnificat every year as he set out); and stags on the high tops, and the odd snipe flipping away, and the blaeberries near where the burns tumble. There were always enough birds to keep everyone happy, somebody always brought along a totally uncontrollable dog and the whole line would halt to watch the proceedings, there was the occasional adder sunning itself by the ancient sheep fanks and, at the end of the day, there was a prize for the wearer of the most ticks.

One of the best bits of the day of course was the picnic lunch, which would meet us at the appointed place brought out by the big white pony with panniers on her back. Someone would have picked some blaeberries on the way up, there was lots of plonk, and beer cans cooling in the burn, and what our nice neighbour would always refer to, whatever it was, as 'Ah, the Perfect Spread', in tones of Berry & Co.

But the *very* best bit of this picnic was, undoubtedly, the moment before it happened: the moment when you had seen the pony ahead of you, with her panniers of goodies; you were exhausted and hungry, you threw yourself down on the ground and lay there in blissful anticipation as you listened to the buzz of conversation, the keepers chunnering, the dogs panting . . . It was just at such a moment that I managed one of my most spectacular mishaps.

We had been doing what was charitably known as the Long Walk, a gruelling huge sweep of hills which involved a very extended first half of the day with a late picnic scheduled for about half-past two, by which time we would have reached the top of the big glen: the pony, and the lunch, would have been brought out in the horsebox on to the track road in the glen below from whence, once saddled up, it was a fairly easy pull for her straight up the hill. We had reached our agreed rendezvous a little early, it was most fiendishly hot, guns and keepers flopped down, groaned a little and unlaced their boots. No one spoke very much, as no one had enough energy to speak. Looking down the hill we could see the pony-man and the great white pony enthusiastically churning up through the heather bloom. Five minutes passed, the sun beat down, the flies buzzed, there was an eagle overhead and some ravens tumbling over each other, and the squeak of the leather harness and the magic sound of clinking bottles in the

panniers could be heard proceeding slowly up the hill towards us.

I was due to leave the party at a quarter to three, make my way down the hill, take the Land-Rover and go off to the airport to meet some guests who were arriving on the afternoon 'plane. My watch had packed up so, in order to be sure of the time, and in case I had to leave the line before arriving at our luncheon spot, I had tied a kitchen clock onto a piece of string around my waist, one of those nice old ones, with a bell-dome on top and huge feet. Just at the moment when the pony appeared in front of us, and everyone had gently started to stir, and people were saying things like Here We Are Then and Saved At Last and Jolly Well Done Bobby to the pony-man, who was removing his cap to wipe his pouring brow, and I was getting to my feet to help unpack the panniers off the heaving white flanks, just at that moment, from the regions of my waist, the alarm went off.

Those old kitchen clocks have rather fine alarms — none of your silly little digital bleeps but good, fully-fledged, raucous, strident, stunning crepitations, a veritable ironmongery of sound. The effect on the pony was electric. She threw up her head, knocked over her minder, gave one piercing whinny of terror, turned on her back legs and took off without more ado, downhill and at the most astonishing speed — ropes and harness flying, the panniers flapping open and bouncing on her huge white rump, encouraging her to even greater effort. Beer cans, salads, cake, game pies and bottles, glasses, baps and picnic boxes, chickens and apples and hard-boiled eggs and tomatoes and salts and ham and

47

bananas and biscuits and the Stilton cheese took off, like an amazing display of culinary fireworks, behind her.

There was a stunned silence, which could have been measured in milliseconds, then everyone began shouting at once, yelling in despair at the vanishing white tornado (she must have been 60 yards downhill by now, and going like the clappers) as the pony-man started running and tumbling after her, hanging on to his cap. The dogs thought this was just perfection and joined in the chase, people were moaning like souls in torment, rolling on the ground and holding their sides, the keepers laughed till they cried and there, standing on top of a peat hag, was one incredulous husband, mouth open, unable to utter. Finally he turned and stalked over to me. I wasn't sure whether to stand my ground or not. 'WHY . . . WHY . . . ?' he yelled, as if I'd been where he was obviously wishing I was by then, somewhere in outer perdition, 'WHY CAN'T YOU WEAR A WRISTWATCH LIKE ANYONE ELSE?'

I made the 'plane, by a whisker.

Over the Hill

August is the month when Heathrow airport is full of immaculately dressed visitors in male groups, clutching huge rifle-cases and large designer carry-alls into which they have stashed their guns, and pronouncing Scottish place-names as if they were mouthwash. August is also the month when I begin to panic: out come the bicycle-exercising machine, the books on Canadian aerobics; the dog is worn to a frazzle from unwonted forced marches and stairs get taken three at a time, all in a frenzied attempt to strengthen the leg muscles. Like Jerome K. Jerome, who admitted that the only athletic sport he ever mastered was backgammon, I am, as always, out of condition — and the stalking season has arrived.

You can stalk all over the world — in Bulgaria, where you are fed sausage and cucumber and whisky before you set off; in Argentina, where you sally forth with a horse, a tent and a couple of guides and disappear into the mountains for a week, to return with a Gold Medal head; in Norway, where you do it at a run, all day, and end up with a moose the size of a barn ambling past you; you can stalk in Ulan Bator, or New Zealand, or Alaska or Kashmir, but there is something indefinably magic about stalking in Scotland. 'I had just returned from India', wrote the Marchioness of Breadalbane in 1907, 'and the men were never tired of listening to stories of sport in the jungle, and of the manner of such things in the Far East; but it always ended with the same paean that, after all, there is no country like Scotland, and no sport like stalking.'

The Marchioness was a fantastic shot, took two dogs out on the hill, and wore a long tweed skirt for stalking together with a sort of flat-topped hat which looked like something more commonly found around the Khyber Pass. What she wore in India is unrecorded, but I imagine it was equally as eccentric for, it is worth noting, should you think of shooting anything anywhere abroad, you will end up taking more luggage, changes of clothes and paraphernalia than you ever dreamed possible in order to look halfway passable for your sartorially exquisite hosts. There was reputedly one Maharajah who would go out after tiger wearing a stiff white collar and striped shirt in order to make his English guests feel more at home. Shoots abroad are undoubtedly Smart.

This, of course, is not the case when stalking in Scotland. In Scotland, a gentleman is perfectly attired for a day on the hill in his grandfather's tweed plus-eights and jacket, a prep-school tie, a pair of army boots, preferably with the old Indian puttees, and a thumbstick. This, together with some ancient form of headgear ('M'father's, actually') combine to make him look like a rather dubious transaction out of *Exchange and Mart*. If you turn up to stalk with him wearing the wrong colour for the hill or, worse still, a Barbour, he will explode: 'Bloody silly thing that, makes a row, looks black in the rain, take it ORF.' He is also scathing about foreign tenants, the Red Deer Commission, women shots and, above all, any high-powered rifle with a telescope sight.

'Not an officer's weapon' he will snort. 'If you can't get
within sixty yards of a beast you shouldn't shoot. If you
can't shoot over proper sights, you're no gentleman.
Told the boy, you use one of them damn' things, I'll
disinherit you. Made him think, I can tell you.' His own
firearm, given to him By The Tenants of the Estate for
his Coming of Age in 1929, according to the worn silver
disc on its stock, is badly in need of re-barrelling and
the wood looks as if it has been gone over by the
rotavator.

Continental shots turn up for a week's stalking in
Scotland lodened up to the eyeballs, the hired minibus
swaying precipitously round the glen road, filled to
bursting with sporting equipment, bags, matching cases
and voluminous green coats. (At one lodge, an extra
ghillie is employed when Germans or Austrians come
stalking, to follow behind carrying the lodens.) They set
out for the hill in suede breeches and boots fit for the
ascent of the North Face, carrying leather rucksacks
containing at least five sweaters of differing weights,
and have pretty plaited slings on their superb, cosseted
rifles. Tenants or guests, they are almost always beautiful shots, having been weaned on roe deer at 400 yards
and chamois (standing shot) at a mile. None of this
carries any ice at all with the local stalkers, who put
foreign guests through their paces in no uncertain
manner before finally thawing out. 'So I said to him
look here feller, I dinna give a damn what ye've shot
before, heere on my ground ye do as I say an if ye dinna
like it ye can just b—— off. After that the mannie was
jus' fine, so I gave him the auld royal . . .'

A few years ago we were invited to shoot in Austria. It

was, distinctly, Smart: the castle corridors were bristling with vast antlers, the dinner was served by liveried footmen, and every rifle in the gun-room was inlaid with gold. I was introduced to the *Jaegermeister* the first morning, and we set off into the dawn to climb the surrounding mountains. We stalked up through the snow line, we waited, we climbed some more, we sat in high seats, we waited, we stalked through woods and over bare screes and waited and finally we returned, having seen nothing. We were there for four days. After each morning's and evening's sortie the party would gather again in the castle and tell their tales of roe, wild cat, lynx, chamois and red deer, of shots taken or missed, of triumphs or disasters — except for me, who had still seen nothing. And there is nothing quite so depressing as sitting for hours in a high seat, next to a very chic and clearly desperate loden-suited head keeper, with whose language you are not totally conversant, while his small brown dog waits patiently below sitting by a rucksack, and seeing nothing, BUT NOTHING, for four days. Lots of midges in the evening air, and birds calling, and wonderful sunrises, but apart from that, nothing.

On the last evening we were all gathered as usual in the library for drinks before dinner and the daily report to our host by the head keeper, who by that time could barely lift his eyes from the floor, while we talked sadly of our departure the next morning at 9 o'clock to catch a 'plane home. Our host joined us finally, full of apologies that I had still had no luck; but, he said, if I would get up early again the following morning, I might have one last chance: the keeper knew of one old stag which might, possibly, make an appearance. If he wasn't there by 8 we could return to the castle, I could change and we could still leave by our 9 o'clock deadline.

The following morning I duly rose at dawn, and set off again with the keeper for the mountains. We climbed into a high seat facing another bit of hill, and waited. At 7.53 the keeper nudged me, smiled for the first time, and pointed up the hill; and there, emerging like some great ghost from the trees, was the biggest stag I had ever seen in my life. I gulped and began to shake and, whispering, started to protest that no, he was too big, and no, I couldn't possibly shoot, and no, thank you very much but really . . . The keeper, who had been arguing with me *sotto voce*, clearly reached desperation point. He stood up, turned to me, and screamed 'SHOOT'. The stag stopped in amazement, and I shot.

So it was that I got a trophy head. We returned to the castle with the keeper leaning on the horn and yelling like a lunatic through the village, and everyone hung out of the windows and shook dusters, and the champagne came out and we missed our plane and a stag that was clearly being kept for some VIP to shoot the following week was given to me merely because I had had no luck for four days.

It is a huge head, and my greatest pride. In his book *Hunting in the Olden Days*, William Scarth-Dixon records an incident with the Easingwold Staghounds when, during an extremely long run, the Master asked an old woman he met on Huggate Wold if she had seen the stag. 'Ah knaw nowt aboot t'stag', said the old woman, 'but I seed summat varry like a donkey wi' an armchair on his head, an he wur a lang way afore ye.' The head is, inevitably, known as the Donkey.

Covert in Confusion

From a man's point of view, the Good Old Days were those in which he, the Great Hunter, left the cave early in the morning and, having spent the day chasing his prey and doing his own thing, did not see his woman until sundown. He can of course do more or less the same thing nowadays, merely by going off to the City or wherever during the week; but the rub comes on Saturdays when your average up-to-date, spoiled and totally unreasonable woman wants to prove her equality by joining him even during daylight hours. Thus we have what in the modern idiom is known as 'The Saturday Shoot'.

Man is born unto trouble, even as the sparks fly upwards. Even unto his Saturdays. But if the woman of his life wishes to partake of what is, has been and always will be the Man's World of Shooting, then she must do so wholeheartedly, selflessly, pulling her weight as part of the team. If going off for a day's shooting takes on the semblance of the Kalahari tribe on the move, then it is her privilege to be the mover: the teamwork involved in ensuring that everything goes smoothly for his day will nevertheless require his help, and this is unstintingly given: 'Haven't you packed up the car YET? Come ON, we're going to be late, of course there's room, just dump it in the back, mind the seat, no not like THAT the big one has to go underneath, leave room for the dog there; what? then you'll just have to take them out

56

and find it, no I don't know where the boots are for God's sake, where's my flask, careful with those cartridges, MIND OUT; no you don't have time now you'll have to go later, where's the dog got to, dammit I can't do EVERYthing . . .'

Once in the shooting field, things aren't much better. 'No not there, THERE, here, put the bag down, no I want the dog there, no I need that for the moment, you stand if you're meant to be loading. Ah, here we go . . . and another, quick, load, LOAD damnit; I can't help that, just take those silly gloves off; did you mark that one, quickly . . . what? sorry but that's really your fault if you will stand in the wrong place; cartridges, NOW; LOOK OUT . . . oh well, you'll just have to pick them up and I'll do it myself.'

By lunchtime the morning nerves have calmed down a bit and he is more relaxed — lots of cheerful banter about wiping the old Colonel's eye, excellent food and drink, and the women doing a good job of handing things round and seeing everyone's all right. She has made up a bit for the earlier, shaming *débâcle* by marking down an old cock on the far side of the river, and he is feeling much better having got a couple of real screamers off that high bank.

In the afternoon it pelts with rain, but as he has very sensibly sent her off to sit behind someone else, he can at least concentrate properly. The dog is behaving beautifully and doesn't miss a thing, and it was lucky he'd remembered to bring the flask, does keep the cold out nicely.

The end of the last drive: just time for a quick cup of tea laced with a little something and then to pack up the car for home. Everything is sodden but at least she has towelled down the dog; she had to give the tea a miss but anyway she's doing the driving which means he can have forty winks on the way back and be in good shape by the time they get home; then she will see to the stuff in the car and sort out the birds and everything and he will feed the dog and have a bath and then they'll be ready for the people coming over for dinner.

It's the teamwork that counts.

Highland Fling

'The proper way to go to Scotland for the first time', my father had told me, 'is to go by train', and so I did. It was a Friday, and October, and the sleeper pulled out of King's Cross full of jovial figures wearing either mow-able tweeds, or kilts with what appeared to be scimitars in their stockings, and English gentlemen in City suits, weighed down with gun-cases, and all saying things like 'Last year we got three-fifty the first day'. It was like going to the Alamo.

I found I was sharing a sleeper with a nice little old lady in a hat who, from the moment I stepped into the compartment, talked non-stop in an accent which I later learned to recognise as Peeblesshire (South, Extra Dry) but which for the first hour or two might just as well have been Bulowayan. Undeterred by my silence she didn't draw breath and, as I finally got the hang of it, I discovered she was giving me a blow-by-By-Blow account of the history of her family, into whose bosom she was thankfully returning after a 'tairrible long' absence — some five days — in the south. On and on she went, as we thundered into the night. Next morning dawned and, still in full spate and hat, she rattled on while I watched my first miles of Scotland hurtle past. At last the train began to slow down, and as we drew into the first stop the guard's cheery Scots voice, Rs rolling like marbles, could be heard approaching down the corridor as he whooshed open each compartment

door and slammed it shut again, announcing the name of the station. Whoosh. ' . . . Forfar'. Bang. Whoosh. 'This stop fer Forfar.' Bang. 'Who's fer Forfar?' Bang. His beaming face appeared round our door. 'Any of yous fer Forfar?' Bang, 'Anyone fer Forfar? . . .' 'Passengers fer Forfar . . .' in diminishing tones down the corridor. The little old lady and I sat, at last, in silence. The whistle blew, the train started up again, and as we pulled slowly out of the station she leaned over to me conspiratorially. '*Well,*' she said, 'Did ye ever hear such cheek? I was for Forfar myself right enough, but I cairtainly wasn't going to let on to *that* nosy divil.'

There are moments in Scotland when the most mundane aspects of life take on an almost surreal quality. If even half the things said by the Scots were said by anyone else, you'd think you'd gone mad. Perhaps it is their form of lateral thinking. Perhaps it's the peat, or the light, that brings out such breathtaking logic; perhaps it's just the whisky in the air.

The old distillery custom of two free drams per worker per day — to be consumed neat on the premises before leaving — is no longer allowed (just as well, too: the men would go blithely riding off into the sunset, which isn't all that far when you think that distilleries are built about 6 feet back from the sea cliffs, on the islands at any rate). But good habits die hard and, even if its is no longer doled out free nor is it the crystal-clear 120° proof spirit straight out of the vats, it is after all still the Water of Life. And people are naturally hospitable: a visit at any time to any croft will elicit the same warm welcome at the door: 'Och, it's you mum, come in, will you have tea or would you rather take a refreshment?'

The doctor's surgery is filled each morning with the regular bleary faces, victims of the previous night's celebrations. 'Morning Sandy, morning Willy, morning Jock, morning Archie', like a club. Willy did explain one day that 'after a coupla jars' thing just happened to him that didn't seem to happen to other people: roads petered out as he wove his way home, corners of buildings would jump out and bite him, mechanical objects assumed a mind of their own. But nobody thinks any the worse of a man who has a thirst on him. Willy indeed was something of a local hero, having spent most of the war in Italy where he had learned many things, including the language. Night after night, Willy's strong tenor could be heard wafting up the hill, construing its way through '*O Sole Mio*' before he passed out in the ditch. 'Wha' a man' they'd say admiringly every morning, as he would be seen holding his head in his hands and leaning on the doc's door. 'By jinks, them natives must have been somethin' for him to know the lingo so well, eh Willy?'

One year the Royal Marine Commandos arrived to do a week's exercises, living rough out on the hill, scavenging, poaching and fending for themselves. The most clued-up participants bivouacked within sight of cottages or farms and were then tended surreptitiously — strictly against orders — by the farmers' wives, who put out baps, stews and small unlabelled bottles on the back porch. One evening a sortie was arranged between the Marines and the locals who had volunteered as territorials: there were various positions — bridges, the Post Office and such-like — to be captured or held. About 3 in the morning I was awakened by a tremendous din going on below in the port which was being held, apparently successfully, by the home team; firecrackers were let off, blanks were fired, then the voice of the postman (unmistakable, as he stuttered) yelling in triumph: 'Lie dddddown ya bbbbbugger, y're ddddead'.

When not in the throes of such emergencies, the tempo of life is fairly relaxed. We were staying away on the West Coast for a week's stalking, during which time a few minor repairs were taking place in the house. Gales of laughter erupted from the kitchen at regular intervals throughout the day, as the participants caught up on the latest gossip between mugs of tea. One afternoon there appeared to be a Slight Problem. 'Ah dinna fash yerself' was the cook's advice to the local painter who, being colour blind (it couldn't happen elsewhere), had just finished painting a large wardrobe in our host's dressing-room a fine shade of pillar-box red, under the mistaken assumption that the word 'VARNISH', scrawled by someone on the outside of the tin, actually referred to its contents. 'Himself'll never notice, though I'm thinking that if I were you I'd mebbe take a stroll out the time he's coming back'. Our host, a fine man but prone to the occasional sense-of-humour failure, duly returned — very late — from a long and wet day on the hill. We all hid under the stairs as he stomped up to his dressing-room, and waited to hear what would happen. When the house had stopped reverberating, the cook extracted herself from behind a sofa — 'Well, the Laird'll be feelin' a wee bitty better now, no doubt' — and disappeared happily.

Back at home again, one weekend a farmers' meeting

was held in the village hall 'to encourage', the Chairman announced, 'forthright views from the maimbers'. Forthright they certainly were. In the middle of a fierce argument concerning lamb counts, a voice was heard growling at the back 'Och, he's a tairrible liar that man. How can he have one hundred per cent lambing, *an him with only eighty sheep?*'

After one apparently appalling dinner at Dalwhinnie, Queen Victoria wrote miserably: 'No pudding, and no FUN.' She obviously moved in the wrong circles.

Two in the Bush

I've been shot round four times, one way and another: by my mother in Kildare, by a Belgian in Wiltshire, by a German in Argyll and by a Spaniard in France.

The incident with my mother really wasn't her fault (I was seven, we were out on the bogs, she didn't notice I had lagged behind with the Siamese cat who liked to come snipe shooting with us, he got a thorn and yowled, she whipped round thinking it was me, and the gun went off). The Belgian, though, got thoroughly over-excited when a roe-buck rushed out between us during a pheasant drive and let fly with both barrels but, distracted perhaps by my yell, missed and felled a small sapling. The German didn't draw blood either, but my Barbour was never the same after; and the Spaniard later remonstrated that, to be perfectly fair, he was merely trying to shoot a duck which had steadfastly refused to fly and which had, rather sportingly I thought, made it on foot through the line to the shelter of my stand.

Perhaps because of all this, I was never a very good shot. I was the most perfectly *safe* shot, mostly due to the fact that I was so terrified of missing, or shooting dangerously, that I ended up never letting off the gun at all. 'But you must have had something come over you' an incredulous host would exclaim, as I'd stand there looking professional with nothing to pick up. And I would shift miserably from one foot to the other and explain that yes, indeed, there had been a lot of birds, masses actually, but I hadn't been *quite* sure about the beaters coming down that slope in front, or the gun on my left, but it had been the most marvellous drive; when in fact I'd spent the whole time praying that nothing would come out and I'd be spared the indignity of missing it.

And on the odd occasion when I did try, I missed some wonderful birds too — before I got the hang of the thing and gave up shooting with a gun altogether. Magical great capercaillie, flying silent and fast over the pines, of which the only thing I could claim was one tail feather (though Pocohontas would have approved); and duck by the zillion when we went flighting in Holland, out in boats before dawn with a keeper bearing schnapps and sausages, and everyone ran out of cartridges while the birds poured over again and again and again; and grouse over the Welsh hills, when I know for certain that the only thing I hit all day was a bumble bee that got in the way of the shot; and even more grouse missed walking up, as I was always frightened of setting the safety catch off by accident, churning over peat hags . . .

Probably the worst time of all was when I was asked to shoot in Spain. It started by our having a Spaniard to stay in Scotland, and taking him out goose flighting. He smoked cigars all the time, and had been totally nonplussed by the lack of 'proper' decoys, explaining how in Spain if you wanted to shoot quail you put out a cage with a blinded bird in it which would call down all its friends and you thus shot 'hundereds of birrrds'. As this was the West Coast, however, the keeper didn't take a blind bit of notice and, having dumped him unceremoniously in a half-filled ditch by the sea wall, muttered something uncomplimentary in Gaelic, told him on no account to move, placed the other guns, and then came to sit with me at the furthest end of the shore where we could tell stories and investigate the mussel beds. Shortly before dawn the flight began and, over a period of three-quarters of an hour or so, something upward of 20,000 geese flew over the Spaniard in his ditch. The sunrise was spectacular, the noise of the barrage, the brilliant flashes emanating from his barrels and the continuous and resounding Spanish expletives were stupendous, and not a thing came down. The other guns were having more success, I was happy on my tussock, when a pair of geese came over me. 'Go on, mum' hissed the keeper, 'and again', and by some inexplicable chance I got my first right and left.

Several minutes later the Spaniard came plashing through the wet sand, his cigar a wreck and his eyes swivelling. 'Neber, neber haf I seen such a shooting; *madre de puta*, eet ees fantaHtic. You will come and shoot in Espain, yes? Ees incredible you will see, for a shooter like you no problem . . .' He went burbling on like something possessed, I made all the right noises and then explained, enunciating carefully, that this had been pure fluke, that really I was a rotten shot and that it would never happen again, ever, and why didn't we all go back now for breakfast as everyone must be famished? But all day long he went on about it, and the upshot was that by the evening we had been formally invited to shoot with him near Toledo and, despite all protests, I was to bring along two guns as well. I didn't have a pair? No problem, for you one is enough, yes? Ha.

67

We went the following November. It was indeed an incredible shoot; beautiful contryside smelling of *jara*, an impressive guest list which seemed to include most of the crowned and uncrowned heads of Europe, lunch in a huge tent with waiters from the Jockey Club of Madrid in white gloves, lots of Rioja, wonderfully presented birds in their hundreds, and perfect sunshine. I hadn't been able to sleep a wink all night but the first drive went off passably enough: the *secretarios* assigned to load, pick up and generally look after me were cheerful and funny, I hadn't made a complete ass of myself, and I was just thinking how marvellous it would be if I could stop, now, while I was still winning, when, as if in answer to prayer, the firing-pin broke.

As I had been using my solitary 16-bore, and as they don't seem to exist in Spain, I knew I could not possibly be offered the loan of a replacement. Relief and elation fought behind an apologetic exterior: *so* sorry, *how* stupid, never mind . . . But no. 'No no, there is no problem, the Prince he has many 20s, he will lend you one, yes? And all the leetle *cartuchas* so you can go on, fantaHtic eh?' and the next drive began.

As the Prince had arms like a baboon the gun didn't appear to fit at any known point. The birds started coming, I lifted the gun and pulled the trigger, and the world exploded. When I had picked myself up and removed the dust, I realised that the leetle *cartuchas* had been specially built by some explosives expert to enable HRH to shoot things out of range to any normal mortal. From then on, it could only get worse. I didn't hit a thing for the rest of the day — not from want of trying either.

My neighbours were polite and busy with their own affairs, and the *secretarios*' cheerful banter died away as they crouched silent and despondent at my feet. At the first toot of the horn which signalled the end of a drive, everyone else's *secretarios* would set off like slipped greyhounds, shouting and tackling each other and roaring with laughter as they picked, scrounged and stole all the birds they could lay their hands on, whether belonging to 'their' gun or not; mine shuffled about disconsolately spitting out olive stones. Finally one of them, a real gentleman, turned to me with all the enthusiasm he could muster: 'Don't worry *señora*, I steal two birds now from game cart, I bring next drive, I put in bush and I find after, OK?' OK? I could have kissed him.

Finally it was the last drive. I was aching in places I never knew existed, my jaw had been dislocated and was now indigo with added lumps, and I knew that if I tried to fire once more my head would split open like a coconut. I let off one agonised, despairing shot into the middle of a cloud of things overhead, and down came a magpie. My *secretarios*, to a man, detonated to their feet yelling like banshees, kissed one another, banged me on the back, cheered like a whole football stadium. Apparently there was a mammoth reward for the team whose gun killed the first magpie in the final drive, and I had saved their day, and my honour.

That evening our host, cigar still hoisted, could talk of nothing else. 'FantaHtic the magpie eh? But poor your face, this stupid gun no good, I find you another . . . don't worry you see tomorrow . . . NO? So, no problem if you no shoot tomorrow, you relax and enjoy . . .' Spaniards are wonderful.

Since I've given up shotguns, being invited to a shoot is now really fun. I sleep well the night before, I don't have to rush off behind a bush before the first drive, I pick up almost as well as a *secretario* and I love every minute of the day. And what they say about a bird in the hand is true, too.

Eating Humble Pie

According to the dictionary, 'eating humble pie' is a phrase which originated 'in the Middle Ages, and the days of venery and the chase'; once the stag had been caught and killed, the best portions of the carcase were kept for the tables of the nobility; the remainder — the offal and the innards, known as the numbles — was given to the hunt servants and the peasantry who could then treat themselves, not to a fine haunch of venison to which they were not entitled, but to *numble pie*, as befitted their lower social standing. The corruption of the word to 'humble' was, etymologically (and socially) speaking, perfectly logical.

Now just as no man, according to the great and good Izaak Walton, is born an angler, so no woman is born a cook. I was not born a cook. I actually dislike cooking; if God, as they say, had wanted me to be a cook He would not have invented restaurants. But I do know how to read a recipe, and there are hordes of good cookbooks around (I once found a marvellous ancient volume written by a stalker's wife, in which were explained the many and amazing things you could do with even the most appalling bits of a stag) — so I can make some sort of stab at the thing, aided by liberal amounts of luck and a heavy hand with the wine bottle. In the savage Middle Ages, when peasants were peasants and ate numbles, things may have been different, but it does seem strange that nowadays, in this enlightened era of Cooking Made Easy, we should find ourselves quite often having to eat the most extraordinarily unappetising dishes in the sacred name of 'game'. I know, of course, how deeply unappetising all these things are in their raw state: awful bedraggled bodies with poor thin feet lying in the sink — 'There you are darling, couple of birds, won't take you a jiffy . . .' — or a beast being gralloched, which does absolutely nothing for anyone's ideas about *nouvelle cuisine*; or even the first time that, having actually caught a trout, I decided I was going to do the whole thing properly myself, turned on the tap, took a deep breath and made the decisive slit, only to find the thing was riddled with maggots . . . I know all that; but the fact that grown-up men complain loudly at home if their egg is half a second overcooked, and the next moment are contemplating someone else's Boulder of Venison with complete equanimity simply because it is 'game' and therefore (surely) inherently delicious, beggars belief.

I remember one incredible weekend in Scotland, where we had been asked to join a stalking party late in the season. It was freezing cold, and the weather was foul: we came off the hill that night blinded by horizontal rain and sleet and aching for a hot bath. Our host, a genial man often to be heard grumbling about the filthy food at Westminster or the club servants who weren't like the ones in the old days, lived in peerless splendour in the main house together with the keeper and the keeper's unmarried daughter who 'did', and the guests were put out in bothies a little way down what was known as 'the drive', a rough road which clung perilously to the vertical and which gave every appearance of having been systematically mined. There was no heating in the bothies, and the water, lovely peaty-brown as it rushed noisily out of the huge old taps, had obviously not gone through any sort of heating system before reaching its destination.

The night was colder than charity; the rain sheeted down, I was glad I'd remembered to bring extra thermals, and we hurried up the drive holding down Barbours over our heads with one hand and me holding up long skirts with the other ('changing for dinner, hope you don't mind, like to keep up the standards a bit'), and stumbling into the huge pot-hole lakes which were, of course, invisible in the dark. Arriving at the main house lashed and sodden, we found our host in a kilt standing in front of an unlit fire in the cavernous drawing-room, glumly trying to fish something out of the bottom of his glass. The dusty eyes of decaying stags' heads peered down from every available wall, the wind screeched triumphantly between the windowpanes into the billowing curtains, old copies of *Sporting Life* took off like gulls, and we stood about dripping and shivering as I realised that the strange gurgling noise I could hear every so often emanated from my shoes.

'Girl's left something in the warming thing' our host announced encouragingly after fifteen minutes, during which time we had gulped down whisky in the forlorn hope that it might frighten the cold. We squelched down a corridor to the dining room. The girl — who was even now, it transpired, sampling the delights of the local shepherd and his pie in the gate-house — had indeed left something in the warmer. Several hours earlier, by the look of it. The T had been boiled out of the

stock soup, the cabbage had taken on the ghastly hue of the drowned and, in a lovely old silver dish, lay something which appeared to have once been a flayed goat. The candles dripped stubbornly over the table, flaring crossly at the wind coming from under the door, and a large dog kept on making strangled noises in a corner and then throwing up what looked like hairy and rather evil old tennis balls. 'Been up at the game larder again have we?' our host said fondly, as the dog lay there reverberating from yet another herculean expectoration. 'Silly old fool'.

Of course this is not the norm. There are the memorably wonderful house parties; the delicious food provided by thoughtful and imaginative and long-suffering and incredible hostesses; the huge roaring stews and seemingly inexhaustible supplies of Good Ordinary Claret for shooting luncheons; the delectable ambrosial things brought out in hampers on the grouse moors; those lovely fat, fresh baps full of mouth-watering goodies that you find wrapped up in your pocket when you're out stalking; and the marvellous cosy evenings and delicious dinners after a day on the hill. These are unforgettable — but so are the numbles.

Have Gun, Will Travel

At a dinner party once, I found myself sitting next to a Frenchman who was, apparently, a famous international shot. The conversation around the table turned to shooting, and it wasn't long before he had everyone's attention, holding forth happily about where he had been, what the bags were, which medal heads he had shot and so forth. The girl on his other side, a lovely and totally non-sporting female, was riveted. 'You mean you can shoot something, somewhere, all year round?' she asked. This was the perfect conversational gauntlet: he began to explain how, for the dedicated sportsman such as himself, the year started, say, in August, when you shot grouse in Scotland; then in September you went to Mongolia for sheep; October was for partridges in Spain, November for moose in Norway, and so on. Doves in Mexico (*'Ah, que c'est gai'*), bear in Alaska, geese on the Hortobagy Plain, chamois in Austria, red deer in Bariloche ('after the carnival in Rio, *bien sûr*'), snipe in Kashmir, and so forth, through all the calendar months. And then, *voilà* (turning with a devastating smile to the girl next to him) it was August again, and Scotland of course. 'But' she finally asked, in the silence that followed this litany, 'do you mean to say you do nothing except shoot? Don't you do any work?' There was a short pause, then he turned to the rest of the table and shook his head in what was obviously geniune amazement. *'Mais, elle est communiste cette fille, n'est-ce-pas?'*

76

Travel undoubtedly broadens the shooting experience, if not the mind. An article appeared lately in which the writer roundly condemned 'people here [who] still think of all foreigners as over excited caricatures who wear funny hats' and, especially, the author of 'a pernicious little shooting book . . . written in a way that should guarantee we never get properly accepted in the EEC let alone on their shoots'. I very much doubt whether the EEC is going to disbar Britain from the Community on the basis of a shooting book, but I do believe not only that we are as funny to foreigners as they often are to us, on the shooting field and off it, but also that both sides enjoy their own, equally as much as each others', foibles. An Englishman very seriously counting cartridges in the middle of the human explosion that follows any partridge drive in Spain gives the locals there quite as much pleasure as that which we derive from watching the same Englishman, in his own country, looking like the prototype for the joke about hedgehogs and Range Rovers, driving *con brio* and totally out of control into a silage pit. It has nothing to do with nationality and everything to do with the ridiculous.

A sixty-year old Argentinian who, in the early 1980s, had shot the record wild boar in his country — a beast of some 472 kilos — laughed until he cried at the recollection of how, when he had been stalking in Scotland, the keeper kept on producing bits of cotton-grass and then throwing them in the air to see which way the wind was swirling. A superb shot, his command of the English language was, however, not quite good enough to follow the keeper's view of the proceedings. 'He ask me eef I do not also, how he say?, take a beet of fluff wid me when I hunt de wildboar, den he laff like crazy, why?' My Spanish was equally insufficient to explain. And it's not merely the language barrier that makes for memorable moments. 'Say professor, how come dis doe's not got no horns?' enquired an enthusiastic American after doing as he was bid by the stalker and shooting a hummel. 'Dis ain't gonna look so great in de photo album back home . . .' So a fine pair of antlers from an old imperial was later taken down off the gun-room wall, and set up behind the dead beast, so that a suitably impressive photographic record of By the Larder After a Day on the Hill could be sent to the folks in Tennessee.

The Russian Olympic shooting team came over to Bisley one year to see what the NRA was all about and to try the different disciplines, complete with minder in dark glasses of whom it was rumoured that he spoke not a word of English and was KGB. They all fell about at the sight of people shooting Match Rifle at 1,200 yards in the old classical back position (known in America as the 'seemyfeetall position') which, it must be admitted, is a pretty funny sight at the best of times; and thereupon clamoured to be allowed to try for themselves, and ('pliss') also kneeling or standing: 'Een Russia, we do everythink in three positions'. It sounded wonderful. Meanwhile the denizens of Bisley camp were enjoying the fact that the minder, still in dark glasses, had been discovered in an armchair on one of the clubhouse verandahs, deeply ensconced in a copy of the *Financial Times*.

By pure coincidence it was only a few months later that we had joined up on a tour going to Russia — nothing to do with shooting, just simple tourism. We had

checked in the luggage at Heathrow airport and were waiting for the hand-baggage to go through the X-ray machines when my husband, very nobly I thought, told me to leave my face-case with him to deal with and go on ahead into the duty-free bit. I duly went through the frisking gate and was meandering happily around the whisky section when I heard a cry of 'There she is, that's her', looked round and saw three officers of the law bearing down on me, reaching inside their jackets as they ran. Very polite they were, some quiet excuse-me-madam-would-you-mind-just-stepping-this-way, and I was escorted off under heavy guard into a small room, one furious husband in hot pursuit. He had, it transpired, put my face-case into the X-ray machine, it had set all the bleepers going, he was summoned to attend as it was opened for inspection and there, nestling cosily in a small box of hairpins, was Exhibit A, a 7.62mm cartridge case and bullet.

It was, by any standards, an awkward moment. I couldn't for the life of me (not a phrase to be used loosely in the circumstances) think how the thing had got there, you couldn't just say 'so sorry how very silly of me' and then faint, Regency-style; and there was also a husband to placate, justifiably incensed to find himself carrying, through no fault of his own, a lethal piece of ammunition for which he could give no rational explanation except to go burbling on that, as it was quite evident (he trusted) that it was not *his* face-case, it had therefore nothing to do with *him*, yes we did both shoot as a matter of fact . . . Then, as if it explained everything, he laughed happily and came up with the brilliant remark that '*actually*, Officer, she shoots for

Ireland, and' (in a conspiratorial tone) 'at *1,200 yards . . .*'

There were Wanted photographs all round the walls of the little room, and at this point there was a distinct click as someone slid back the safety-catch on their handgun. And then it came to me. The previous week I had, indeed, been shooting the Imperial Meeting at Bisley — a five-day stint which involves living in camp and which therefore justifies, as any lady would agree, the inclusion of a face-case amongst one's affairs. The last evening, after the Elcho Match, is always a little fraught, packing up the car with rifles, suitcases, boxes of ammunition and all the attendant paraphernalia; I had found a spare round in my pocket and had jammed it into the nearest receptacle to hand, which happened to be the box of hairpins I was packing at the time into the face-case, meaning to sort it all out when I got home. It was, indeed the most totally irresponsible thing to have done, and they could have chucked me in a cell and thrown away the key. Especially if they'd only found it on our arrival in Russia.

'And that', he said, half an hour later as we finally emerged, the bullet removed and bagged up and held for Safe Keeping and forms signed in triplicate and general relief all around 'Is the VERY last time I EVER carry ANY of your bags when we're travelling.'

All things considered, it seemed a reasonable enough remark.

A Glossary of Sporting Terms

AEREATED (Adj,. E. Anglia) See AWKWARD below. (As in'The old General 'e don't 'arf get —— when 'e misses a shot.')

AIRLY (Scots) Measurement of time, usually used in connection with goose or duck flighting. 'It's a wee bitty —— yet' implies that as the dawn has not yet broken and it's still pitch black, you should take care what you sit down in.

AWKWARD (adj.) Traditionally the state of mind of the more senior members of any shooting party, usually the result of rather too free a conversation with the port decanter the previous evening. The following formula may be of use: —— + ADDLED + ANNO DOMINI + AEREATED (*qv*) = APOPLECTIC.

BEDDING Somewhat obscure portion of a rifle's anatomy to which a lady should not loosely refer in mixed company. —— SCREWS: *idem.*

BITCH 1) (Noun) The female of the species *Canis.* 2) (Scots) Term of affection usually prefixed by adj. 'auld'. 3) (Verb) For use of this word in the vb mode, see GROUSE below.

BORE Measurement of the internal diameter of the

82

chamber of a shotgun (ie its calibre). (As in 'a 20– —— '
or 'a 16– —— '. Most commonly, reference is made to
'a 12– —— ' or 'a monumental old —— '.)

CAUDAL DISC Creamy patch seen on the rump of
most species of deer which means they've seen you first,
sometimes the result of what irate stalkers refer to as
'Too much damned CHATTER'.

CHAMBER The part of a rifle barrel nearest to the
breech which receives the cartridge when the rifle is
loaded. See note, however, to BEDDING above.

DESOLATE, DRENCHED, DAMP, DAWN, DITCH
Terms frequently employed when flighting geese. See
also DRIVING 2) below.

DRIVE (Noun) Complicated manoeuvre involving the
use of as many of the locals who aren't actually on the
head keeper's hit list, flag-wavers, stick-tappers and
much vocalisation, in order to direct the flight of the
birds over the guns.

DRIVING 1) (Verb) Directing the flight of the birds
etc. It is the head keeper's responsibility to see that the
birds are pushed forward towards the waiting line of
guns in a steady stream; also to ensure that the guns are
kept awake during a 'poor' drive; this accounts for in-
termittent screams of 'Over' or (in winter) 'Wood-
COCK', neither of which need bear the faintest relation
to the truth but which act as aural cosmetics to an
otherwise dull patch. 2) (Adj.) The quality of most rain
during the shooting season.

EJECTION, ELEVATION, EQUIPMENT All rifle shooting terms which should not cause offence to any lady.

ENGLISHMAN This term refers only to a particular breed of partridge. If referring to the male of the human species the correct terminology is 'ENGLISH GENTLEMAN'. Females of the human species are referred to by English gentlemen, generically, as 'women'.

FASH (Scots) Invariably preceded by the word 'Dinna', regularly heard north of the Border by keepers when something spectacularly awful has occurred and One Hell Of A Row is brewing.

FORRARD In front; condensed form of phrase 'There is a bird in front of you so look OUT'. (As in 'Cock ——— ', a phrase which a lady should eschew in favour of 'To your right' or 'To your left' when standing behind an English gentleman.)

FRENCHMAN Usually employed in a pejorative sense (as in 'Damned ——— '), this word in a shooting context refers solely to a certain breed of partridge and is no reflection of the XENOPHOBIA (*qv*) of the host.

GIN ——— TRAPS are illegal. SLOE ——— is not, although King's GINGER is more of a GENTLEMAN's tipple.

GOOD The ultimate accolade of the English gentleman, as in ——— SHOT, ——— SPORT, ——— MANNERS (applied to dogs) and, very occasionally, ——— LITTLE

WOMAN (as in 'Jolly —— little woman you've got there, picks up like anything, hum?').

GROUSE (Noun) (NB: People who use this word in the verb mode are invariably detailed off as walking gun for the day, or sent off the hill, or made to beat the rhododendron drives.)

HILL (Scots) 1) Elsewhere in the kingdom the same geophysical feature would be referred to as mountain, tor, bluff, crag, peak, K2 etc. 2) WEE —— applies to any mountain peak under 2,000 feet.

HI-LOST Repetitious cry of an anxious nature emanating from bushes etc. after a drive as bemused dogs, who have spent the rest of the year happily retrieving slippers from under the bed, are frantically urged to find, pick and bring to hand a bird which their owners feel sure they have hit. Keepers' dogs, who know the form, perform this to the single command 'In-there-ya-bugger'.

HURDIES (Scots) Literati who are lovers of R. Burns Esq., or the unfortunate out-of-condition lady stalking guest who is bidden to 'Shift yer —— , wifey', will know this to be a Scottish term for the proximal segment of the vertebral leg extending from the hip to the knee, more commonly known as the buttocks.

ILL In the context of sporting matters, this word does not denote sickness but, always hyphenated to a suffix, invariably refers disparagingly to someone else of whom the speaker (an English gentleman) roundly disapproves. As in 'an —— BRED, —— CONDITIONED, —— —— ASSORTED sort of fella, shoots with fancy foreign cartridges, if you get my drift'.

IMPERIAL An exceptionally fine stag always standing 20 feet on the other side of the MARCH (*qv*).

IRON TARGET Ritual humiliation to which the prospective stalking guest is submitted by the stalker before setting off for the HILL (*qv*), at the termination of which the invariable comment is 'Well, that'll just have to do then'.

JAG (Noun) Mention of a —— in any context other than that of a cleaning aid for a firearm will result in the speaker's dismissal from the shooting party. An English gentleman does not own any other sort of —— .

KIPPER Regulation breakfast fare to the north-west of the Border, guaranteed to make the rest of the day a complete torture. See also WIND 2) below.

LAIRD (Scots, arch.) Term bristling with connotations of Victorian architecture, tartan, glass-eyed stags' heads hung on baronial walls, stuffed birds under domes and long draughty corridors. If invited to stay and shoot with one, bring thermals.

LEFT (Verb, p.part.) A bird that is —— is one that is usually travelling through the air too high/fast for the comfort of the gun below, who suspects that he will miss it if he fires and does not wish to be thus branded as a Bad Shot. Interestingly, however, the reasons for LEAV-

ING a bird generally bear no relation to this fact. (As in 'It was coming so low that I —— it'; 'Thought it was cocks only' etc.)

MARCH 1) Third month of the Gregorian calender. 2) (Scots) The boundary between Scottish estates, usually designated by something as totally missable as a pile of stones (cairn) and across which the most desirable beasts always vanish mysteriously after any unsuccessful stalk. (As in 'Lost him over the —— '; 'Bit uncertain, that —— , so we decided it was better to be sure than sorry eh?'. This in no way even hints at incompetence and provides a useful excuse for returning home emtpy-handed. The stalker's version of the proceedings usually differs.)

MIDGES The best possible reason for not going out after roe deer, or sea trout, or anything, at dawn or dusk.

MISS (Verb) It is an interesting fact that very few people ever —— (*qv* LEFT above).

MIST A perfectly acceptable reason for not taking a shot, or for MISSING.

MIZZLE A kind of light, fully permeating rain. Not a good reason for not taking shot, or for MISSING.

NEW A somewhat derogatory term in the shooting field where, it must be remembered, everything should be as old as possible (equipment, clothes, participants, money, blood). It is, however, a generally accepted term when used as an apology for lack of excellence. As in ' —— barrels, damned thing won't shoot straight'; ' —— keeper, hasn't quite got the hang of things yet, I'm afraid'; 'I say I'm most frightfully sorry about that, —— dog, first day out, don't you know'.

OFFICER The benchmark, or touchstone, against which excellence is measured. As in 'Marvellous show of birds, real ——'s drive, that'; 'Not quite an ——'s hat'; 'Come back to the house after, got an old bottle of quite good ——'s port'.

88

OVER-AND-UNDER A shotgun the barrels of which are set, not side by side, but one on top of the other, much favoured in clay pigeon competitions. Not an OFFICER's weapon.

PICKING UP The shooting field is the only place in which a lady may indulge in —— with impunity.

PIECE 1) (Noun, arch.) Weapon. 2) (Chiefly Scots) The remnants of something you put in your pocket after breakfast in order to have something to eat at midday when stalking. As this particular sport involves creeping through rivers and burns, and crawling/sliding/scrabbling over rocks/heather/screes, eggs and tomatoes are to be avoided. The stalker will have left his —— in the van, to enjoy later, together with a thermos of sweet milky tea spiced with a clove. If you have performed on the hill to his satisfaction he may offer you some. If not, not.

POINTING Desirable in dogs and buildings, forbidden to children and guns.

QUESTION (Verb) Don't.

RISE 1) (Verb) See AIRLY above. 2) (Verb) Movement upwards of birds flushed out of the heather, woods or ground cover. See DRIVE 1) above. 3) (Noun) The degree of elevation of telescope or open sights on a rifle which raises the point of aim. It is not up to a lady to ask a gentleman what his —— is between, say, 60 and 200 yards/breakfast and luncheon etc.

ROAR 1) The noise made by a stag at the onset of his sexual urge. 2) The noise heard, usually throughout the shooting season, which indicates that a senior member of the party is suffering some minor irritation. Bears no relationship to 1).

ROUND (Noun) Another word for rifle ammunition — nothing to do with public houses.

RUT (Noun) 1) A thing you get stuck in. Not to be confused with 2) the mating season for red deer, when stags are heard to ROAR 1) (*qv*), usually in October.

SABBATH (Orig. Hebrew, Scots in this context) The day on which nothing may be shot. As in 'A good day wasted on the —— '.

SLÀINTE (Scots Gaelic) Word which accompanies drinking after a day's sport. (Sometimes used in conjunction with the exhortation 'More blood').

STALKER The man in front who is the only person able to see what's going on.

TICKS (Pl. noun) Members of the *Ixodoidea* species of parasites. Natural habitat: heather, moors, ferns, tweed etc. Wear as many layers as possible of something impermeable to —— (steel plate?) under your breeches and pretty coloured shooting stockings and proper lace-up hill shoes with leather fringes in front; as gumboots, about the only other thing —— don't latch on to, are Not Worn on a Grouse Moor.

TRAJECTORY (Noun) 1) Path followed by rifle bullet. 2) Path followed by the unwary after firing a shot lying UPHILL (*qv*).

TWELFTH, THE (Noun, often the '**GLORIOUS** —— ') The most famous date in the shooting calendar. Bad news for GROUSE (noun) but good news for TICKS (*qv*).

UPHILL Where anything that you're after invariably is (numbered peg, butt, beast etc.). See also HILL.

VERMICULATED (Adj.) 1) Shotgun barrels usually made of strips or rods of iron or steel coiled in a spiral to form a tube, and having a pattern as if made by the tracks of worms (also known as Damascus or damascened barrels). 2) The appearance of sandwiches found abandoned, long after the shooting season is over, in the pocket of your shooting jacket. *Qv* PIECE above.

WELTSCHMERTZ (German noun) A sense of deep and total weariness which can only be alleviated by taking a deep bath and a large glass of something.

WIND (Noun) 1) One of the many reasons for explaining why a bullet failed to connect with its mark (as in 'Couldn't possibly hold the rifle steady in that —— , of course'), or why a bird was LEFT (*qv*) (as in 'Came screaming off the top of that bank with the —— up their tails, absolutely impossible'). 2) The result of absent-mindedly consuming VERMICULATED 2) above. (Likewise see KIPPER.)

91

X (Letter) 1) Universal symbol for known location. 2) Universal symbol for unknown quantity. 3) Symbol occasionally found in host's private game book against list of guests' names to indicate those who are Never To Be Asked Again.

XENOPHOBIA (Noun, from Greek) Fear or distrust, usually evinced by most elderly English gentlemen and all **OFFICERS** (*qv*), for anything foreign. (As in 'Bloody man turned up wearing one of those damned poofter green cape jobs, might as well have been one of Glubb's Girls, eh?')

YOURS Cry most frequently heard during a driven shoot occasioned by 1) genuinely unselfish desire not to 'poach' a bird which is actually making for the airspace above someone else's head; 2) panic.

ZERO 1) (Verb) To adjust the sighting both vertical and lateral of a rifle, by firing at a mark. (See IRON TARGET above.) 2) (Noun) Numerical symbol denoting absence of quantity. To achieve this as the tally of the day's bag may result in Nemesis. (See X 3) above.)

ZOMBIE (Noun, from Afro-Carib.) 1) Person thought to resemble or to incarnate the walking dead; person brought back to life by witchcraft. 2) Person returning from a day on the HILL (*qv*).